I0106369

How to Resist ICE
in Your Neighborhood and Town

February 2026

Compiled by Bad Penny
An Imprint of Scuppernong Editions

Bad Penny does not assert a copyright to this material.
Please copy at will and/or download the free PDF here:
scuppernongeditions.com/how-to-resist-ice/

If copying, please cite the sources listed.

The print edition is priced at cost, in order to cover the
expense of printing and distributing this information.

First Edition : February 2026
ISBN 978-1-95910-405-6

Bad Penny is an imprint of Scuppernong Editions.

No AI was used in the generation of this work.

Scuppernong Editions
Greensboro, North Carolina
scuppernongeditions.com

All details and instructions are provisional. According to the Trump Administration, all rights are provisional. Future editions will be updated with more current data.

Legal disclaimer
This document is for general informational purposes only. Its contents are not legal advice. If you are in need of legal advice, please contact an attorney.

At Home

As a Business

In the Military / Law Enforcement

US Government Simple Sabotage Manual

WHAT ARE ICE AND CBP?

History

ICE (Immigration and Customs Enforcement) is a division of the Department of Homeland Security (DHS), created by the Homeland Security Act of 2002, passed in the wake of 9/11. The act created DHS and reorganized other agencies, merging the US Customs Service (formerly under the Treasury Department) and the Immigration and Naturalization Service (formerly under the Justice Department) to form ICE.

According to their website, ICE claims its mission is 'to protect America through criminal investigations and enforcing immigration laws to preserve national security and public safety.'

Customs and Border Patrol (CBP) are charged with border security and enforcement at the border and ports of entry. However, these distinctions have become blurry as CBP agents have been moved away from the border to assist ICE, rendering the two organizations often indistinguishable. Both agencies are part of the Department of Homeland Security.

In January 2026, a whistleblower disclosed that a May 2025 memo stated ICE agents may forcefully enter using only administrative warrants signed by an immigration officer (as opposed to judicial warrants signed by a judge, which apply to all other US law enforcement agencies). This statement has not yet been challenged or upheld in a court. CBP, on the other hand, has the authority to conduct searches without a warrant only 'within a reasonable distance' of a US border. A 'reasonable distance' is defined as within 100 miles of a border or coast.

Though the Trump Administration repeatedly states it is only arresting 'the worst of the worst,' according to ICE data, only 29% of all detainees booked between October 2018 and November 2024 had a criminal record in the US. In 2024, 43.8% of detainees with criminal records had been convicted of misdemeanors, 35.2% of felonies, and 17% of aggravated felonies.

SOURCE: USA Facts; *Seattle Times*

Deportations by President

While politicians from both parties have called for immigration reform that could produce a viable pathway to citizenship for those who are presently in the US without documentation, both parties have declined to cooperate in bringing such a plan to fruition, out of the desire to avoid giving a win to its political opponent. Therefore, the fates of those who attempt to follow the rules of the US immigration system have become a political football; for those in elected office regardless of party, it is often more valuable to use ICE or CBP to remove or return those subject to deportation, rather than reforming the immigration system. According to the Office of Homeland Security Statistics:

› **Removals** are the compulsory and confirmed movement of an inadmissible or deportable alien out of the United States based on an order of removal. An alien who is removed has administrative or criminal consequences placed on subsequent reentry owing to the fact of the removal.
› **Returns** are the confirmed movement of an inadmissible or deportable alien out of the United States not based on an order of removal.

Both removal and return are legal means of deportation.

The Obama Administration removed more people, with fewer people returned. The number ranged between 962,306 to 438,175 per year of his administration.

The George W. Bush Administration returned more people, with fewer removed. The number ranged from 1,538,397 to 1,171,058 per year of his administration.

The large majority of the numbers quoted above are returns, thus not involving due process in the US legal system. In general, CBP is involved with returns; ICE is involved with removals.

SOURCE: Office of Homeland Security Statistics

Trump's First Term

On the campaign trail in 2016, Donald Trump outlined a ten-point plan on immigration. Some of these changes were realized during his first administration, while others were carried over to his second.

1. Build a Border Wall
2. End Catch-and-Release
3. Enhance the pursuit of Unauthorized Immigrants Who Have Committed Crimes
4. Crack down on Sanctuary Cities
5. End Obama-Era Programs to Protect Unauthorized Immigrants
6. Introduce Travel Bans and Extreme Vettting
7. Ensure Countries Accept their Deported Nationals
8. Complete the Biometric Entry-Exit Exam
9. "Turn Off the Jobs and Benefit Magnet"
10. Reform the Legal Immigration System

Many of these goals were achieved, or partially achieved, during his first four years in office. The Trump administration deported 1.5 million during his four years in office, primarily returns.

SOURCE: Migration Policy Institute

Biden's Term

However, the Biden Administration removed or returned 775,000 people in Fiscal Year 2024 alone, more than any year since 2010, putting the Biden administration on track to surpass the first Trump administration's numbers. (Complete figures are not yet available.)

SOURCE: Migration Policy Institute

Rhetoric

On the campaign trail and through his administrations, Donald Trump has consistently dehumanized brown and black immigrants, citizens or not, characterizing them as 'rapists,' 'murderers,' 'bloodthirsty criminals,' and 'the most violent people on earth.' He has repeatedly called black and brown immigrants 'animals,' and stated that they are genetically predisposed to commit crimes.

He has wrongly suggested that 'illegal immigrants' receive untold government benefits including 'Welfare' and Medicaid.

This language has been activated to justify much more aggressive ICE tactics than have been used in the past. (*Politico*)

In the first year of his second administration, Trump has stripped hundreds of thousands of Haitian, Venezuelan, and Afghan immigrants of temporary legal status, expanding the pool of people who could be deported.

He has promised to end birthright citizenship in an executive order targeting the US-born children of undocumented mothers and fathers.

During his first year in office, agents have arrested spouses at their green card interviews, pulled people from certain countries out of their naturalization ceremonies moments before they were to become citizens, and revoked thousands of student visas.

A 2025 executive order expressly bans travel from twelve countries—Afghanistan, Burma, Chad, Republic of the Congo, Equatorial Guinea, Eritrea, Haiti, Iran, Libya, Somalia, Sudan, Yemen—and partially restricts travel from seven others—Burundi, Cuba, Laos, Sierra Leone, Togo, Turkmenistan, and Venezuela. The order pulls the rug out from under immigrants who have followed every requirement within the US immigration system, by arguing that they have not been sufficiently vetted.

Trump promises to deport 1 million people a year. (*Reuters*)

Budget

In 2016, the annual budget for ICE was under $6 billion. Thanks to Trump's *One Big Beautiful Bill*, it now has more than $85 billion a year at its disposal, larger than all other federal law enforcement agencies combined.

In July 2025, Congress passed this massive spending package which gave ICE $170 billion through September 2029, over their annual $19 billion annual budget. (*NPR*)

Recruitment

Trump's *One Big Beautiful Bill* significantly increases the number of ICE agents on the street, offering 'unparalleled recruitment incentives' including:

> A starting salary of $51,632 – $84,277 (USAJOBS)
> A signing bonus of up to $50,000
> Up to $60,000 in student loan repayment
> Up to 25% in premium pay

The agency also offers attractive benefits packages, including health, dental and vision insurance; life and long-term care insurance; a retirement plan; eligibility for the Thrift Savings Plan; flexible spending accounts; an Employee Assistance Program; personal and sick leave days; and paid federal holidays. (ICE News)

ICE has used white supremacist and neo-Nazi language in its recruitment efforts. In October 2025, the DHS posted an image of George Washington on horseback on the ICE recruitment page. The tagline was 'America for Americans,' a phrase used by the Ku Klux Klan. (*CBC*)

Lawmakers have voiced concerns over how many ICE recruits were previously associated with neo-Nazi, white supremacist gangs or hate groups. Reporting on this has just started to appear. *The Nation* reports that recruits sent to the Federal Law Enforcement Academy in Brunswick, Georgia were "discovered to have tattoos associated with gangs and white supremacists."

As to how they are hiring, in August 2025, journalist Laura Jedeed attended an ICE Career Expo in Arlington, Texas. One month later, despite failing to complete the required paperwork or participate in a background check, after a 6-minute interview, she received notification that she had been hired by ICE as a deportation officer. She wrote an article for *Slate* about the experience and included screen captures of the notifications. ICE has denied offering her a job. (*The Oregonian*)

Training

Prior to Trump's aggressive ICE recruitment drive, deportation officers received five months of training before being placed in the field. In 2025, that training period was cut to 48 days. (Poynter)

The actual training afforded officers is redacted on ICE websites. An investigation by *Al-Jazeera* found no training in de-escalation tactics, and an emphasis on strategies for evading lawsuits.

ICE officers have the same "qualified immunity" accorded most law enforcement officials, but they do not have legal "absolute immunity" as suggested by Stephen Miller or Vice President J.D. Vance.

Quotas

Trump has set a quota of 3,000 ICE arrests a day, in order to reach his goal of over 1 million deportations a year. (ICE's daily arrest average between January 20 and October 15, 2025, was 891.)

Fueling the larger arrest numbers is ICE's decision to also target people without criminal convictions or charges. This aggressive leap in demanded arrests could account for the indiscriminate and sloppy arrests we see. (*Axios*)

ICE's daily arrest numbers include arrests of US citizens, legal residents, undocumented residents following established immigration procedures, and still others.

Prisons, Private Prisons, and Prisons Outside the US

Conditions in ICE detention centers, whether government operated or privately operated, have continuously been reported as severe and horrific including overpopulation, lack of medical care, lack of basic needs, violation of rights, punitive treatment and harsh conditions. (ACLU)

On his first day in office, Donald Trump reversed a Biden executive order to curb the use of private prisons. Geo Group and CoreCivic are private, for-profit detention companies and they have the largest contracts with ICE to house those arrested and detained. Both have rushed to activate idle facilities and build new ones in the expectation of increasing arrests and detentions by ICE.

Amnesty International reports 'a deliberate system built to punish, dehumanize, and hide the suffering of people in detention' at both Florida's 'Alligator Alcatraz' and Krome Detention Centers. 'Alligator Alcatraz' is run by the State of Florida, Krome is run by Akima Infrastructure Protection. (Amnesty International)

Physicians for Human Rights reports torture and inhuman treatment in ICE detention centers, including those held in for-profit prisons.

At least six people have died in ICE detention centers in January of 2026 alone, following at least 30 deaths in ICE custody last year, a two-decade high. (*Reuters*)

The Trump Administration has deported hundreds to El Salvador's notorious CECOT prison, and promises to deport more, hinting that they could send American citizens there as well. (ABC) This act has widely been viewed as unconstitutional.

Human Rights Watch reports conditions at CECOT "includes cases of torture, ill-treatment, incommunicado detention, severe violations of due process and inhumane conditions, such as lack of access to adequate healthcare and food."

Due Process

The Fifth Amendment to the US Constitution says no one shall be 'deprived of life, liberty or property without due process of the law.' The Due Process Clause in the Fourteenth Amendment extended this obligation to the states. These words are understood to mean that all levels of the American government must operate within the law. (Cornell Law School)

Both the President and Vice President have complained about the judicial requirements of detention and deportation, with Trump suggesting that to give everyone detained a hearing "would take, without exaggeration, 200 years." Vice President Vance has called immigration court 'a fake legal process' and Stephen Miller has stated, "The judicial process is for Americans. Immediate deportation is for illegal aliens." (*NPR*)

The Constitution explicitly states "no person."

Nonetheless, the Trump administration has deported thousands without due process.

In January 2026, Chief Judge for the US District Court of Minnesota Patrick J. Schlitz published a list of almost 100 court orders that ICE had violated that month alone. He wrote that the "extent of ICE's noncompliance is almost certainly understated. This list is confined to orders issued since January 1, 2026, and the list was hurriedly compiled by extraordinarily busy judges." (*Reason*)

Warrantless Stops and Searches

ICE has operated using two kinds of warrants to stop or search a person, vehicle, or home.

› An **administrative warrant** is signed by people who work for the Executive branch, nominally under the supervision of the President.
› A **judicial warrant** is signed by a judge.

The difference between the two on the ground is that judicial warrants allow agents to enter and search a home, or the non-public area of a business, while administrative warrants do not. Judicial warrants require evidence and a third-party arbiter; administrative warrants do not.

In an internal memo issued in 2025, revealed by the complaint of a whistleblower in January 2026, ICE authorizes itself to forcefully enter homes on simply an administrative warrant, thus bypassing the courts altogether.

This directive is widely viewed as unconstitutional, and the courts are beginning to throw out arrests without judicial warrants. (*CNN*)

In Chicago, a judge has already ordered 600 people to be released (*Axios*) because they were arrested without a judicial warrant (with more releases possible).

A judge in Washington, D.C., has also halted warrantless arrests after an enforcement surge drew litigation. (*Axios*)

Detention of Children and Deaths

The Marshall Project reports at least 3,800 children under the age of 18, including 20 infants, have been booked since Trump took office.

Protections are legally provided for children in custody. It is generally interpreted as excessive for a child to be held by ICE for more than 20 days. Lawyers at the Dilley Immigration Processing Facility in Texas, run by CoreCivic, have documented at least five children held for more than five months.

In mid-December 2025, the Trump Administration was holding 68,440 people in detention; nearly 75% had no criminal record.

Thirty-two people died in ICE detention in 2025. Lawyers and immigration experts have raised concerns about lack of medical care, overcrowding, lack of food and water. (*The Guardian*)

At least 9 people have been killed by ICE or died in ICE custody in January 2026 alone (*Al-Jazeera*):

On New Years Eve, an off-duty ICE officer shot **Keith Porter** to death in Los Angeles.

Geraldo Lunas Campos died on January 3 at the Camp East Montana detention facility in Texas. He died from "asphyxia due to neck and torso compression." His death was ruled a homicide.

Victor Manuel Diaz also died in ICE custody at Camp East Montana on January 6. An ICE statement listed the cause of death as suicide, but his body was transferred to the William Beaumont Army Medical Center for an autopsy, instead of the county medical examiner, leading the family to suspect foul play.

Parady La was found unresponsive in his cell at the Federal Detention Facility in Philadelphia. According to ICE, he experienced "severe drug withdrawal" symptoms.

Luis Beltran Yanez-Cruz died on January 6 of "heart-related health issues." His family reported he had been feeling ill for weeks and had only been given pain medication.

Heber Sanchez Dominguez was found dead in his cell on January 14 at the Robert A. Deyton Detention Facility in Georgia. Staff discovered him "hanging by the neck and unresponsive." The lack of details prompted calls for an investigation from the Mexican Consulate in Atlanta.

Luis Gustavo Nunez Caceres died on January 5 after being admitted for "chronic heart-related issues." He had been transferred from the Joe Corley Processing Center in Texas.

Renee Nicole Good was shot 3 times while driving away from ICE officers.

Alex Pretti was shot 10 times while being restrained on the ground in Minneapolis.

ICE Theater

Just after midnight on September 30, 2025, 300 agents from CBP, the FBI and other federal agencies stormed a 130-unit apartment building on the South Side of Chicago. Black Hawk helicopters hovered over the building and SWAT teams rappelled to the roof. Television crews had been invited to film the raid, necessitated by the fact, the Trump administration said, that the building had been taken over by Tren de Aragua, a notorious (to the administration), Venezuelan gang.

The officers knocked down doors and hurled flash-bang grenades while families cowered in their bedrooms.

The Trump administration released, soon after, a Hollywood-production style video of the event that made it look like the trailer for an upcoming action movie. (*x.com*)

Federal officials have released no evidence they found anything illicit in the raid of the building.

Federal prosecutors failed to file a single criminal charge against the 37 people arrested that night and paraded on the street for the cameras. (*ProPublica*)

Recently fired US Border Patrol Commander Greg Bovino has employed a video team to dramatize ICE operations, and he likes to post on social media. In November 2025, he posted a video on Facebook depicting a projection of the ICE logo in the sky, much like the Bat Signal. The narrator states: "When that light hits the sky, it's not just a call. It's a warning." (*The Assembly*)

An Extrajudicial Force

ICE masks its operatives and protects their anonymity by supplying no markings (nametags, badges, etc.) to identify agents.

It detains people without probable cause, including US citizens.

It deports people without hearing and due process, including US citizens.

It does not hold its officers responsible for civilian deaths and refuses any process of investigation.

It uses five-year-old children as bait to lure other family members outside the house. (*The Guardian*)

It invades houses and businesses without judicial warrants.

Attorney General Pam Bondi's offer to Minnesota Governor Tim Walz to withdraw ICE agents from the state if he relinquished Minnesota voter rolls infers ICE is also party to extortion.

ICE is a government agency operating outside the law. It is an extrajudicial force.

RESISTING ICE

Why Resist ICE?

You have your own reasons for resisting ICE. Others have their own reasons. Sometimes these reasons overlap, sometimes they are more distinct. Protests routinely incorporate different people with different goals. As you join in cooperation with members of your community, listen when others discuss why they are resisting ICE and share your own perspective when you feel it is safe to do so. If you are resisting ICE, you are participating in a movement that intends to preserve the safety of those targeted by ICE; at all times, look after your own safety and the safety of others with whom you are working.

ICE Watch Training

ICE Watch is a community structure. Find an ICE Watch training in your area. Become part of an ICE Watch community and help protect your neighbors and the vulnerable within your neighborhood or town. In North Carolina, ICE Watch Training is provided by SiembraNC.

Here are some of the primary functions performed by ICE Watch groups. When you join an ICE Watch in your area, make sure you follow the guidelines provided by your group.

If You Arrive Before the Abduction

› Whistle (a long blast) to alert neighbors.
› Document the **Size**, **Activity**, **Location**, **Unit/Uniform**, **Time**, and **Equipment** (SALUTE).

Size How many agents and how many vehicles? Film and take photos, with an emphasis on the agents, preserving the detainee's anonymity, if possible.

Activity What are the agents doing? If someone you know is detained, note their name, phone number and date of birth, if possible.

Location Exact address or intersection.

Units Document any letters, details or patches on their uniforms, vests, and vehicles.

Time What precise time?

Equipment Did the agents have guns, dogs, battering rams? Document their vehicles.

If You Arrive After the Abduction

› Canvass the area. Speak to loved ones, business owners, and possible witnesses. Try to gather as much of the information above as possible.
› Get video of the abduction. This may be possible from security cameras or the phones of witnesses.

> Respect boundaries. People may be traumatized by what just happened or they may not understand what side you're on. Focus on what you can do to help the detained and their family.

> Contact family. ICE often leaves victim's cars abandoned and unlocked. They may contain the victim's keys, wallet, and other valuables. Often, victims cannot contact their families. (ICE does not contact the families of detainees.) If you can, contact the family and let them know what has happened.

Whistle Protocol

> Short, broken blasts: *I see ICE.*
> Long, continuous blast: *ICE is abducting someone.*
> We want to enable vulnerable people to get inside or away while responders form a crowd.

Report Information and Activity in Chats

> Use the protocols in place in your community to report information in chats.
> If you share information, be a precise as possible. Use the SALUTE formula above.

SOURCE: Crimethinc

Fourth Amendment Workplace

Fourth Amendment Workplace protocols apply to businesses and organizations that may employ or aid at-risk members of your community.

A Fourth Amendment Workplace training will apprise you of your rights as a business or organization in protecting your employees, customers, or the people you serve.

General guidelines can be found in the As a Business section of this book.

Often, the same groups that provide ICE Watch training also provide Fourth Amendment Workplace Training.

What to Do If You or a Loved One Are Detained by ICE

Immediate Steps

1 *Ask your family member/friend for their A-Number (A#)*

   This number usually contains 9 digits.

   ICE will give them this number upon arrest.

   If your family member/friend filed a previous immigration application, it's likely they will already have an A# on any documents from immigration.

   If your family member/friend was arrested at the border and allowed to enter, it's likely they will already have an A# in their immigration documents.

2 *Locating someone in detention*

   You can use this link to locate your family member/friend if they have been detained by ICE. Search by either A# and country of birth, or the person's biographical information: locator.ice.gov/odls/#/search

   ICE has information (including location and contact information) for the detention centers it uses on its website: www.ice.gov/detention-facilities

3 *Communication / Visits*

   Once you locate your family member/friend using the link above, you may contact the detention center to schedule calls or visits. Some facilities allow for in-person visitation while others may provide video-visitation only.

   Each facility has its own process for setting up phone accounts so that your family member/friend can call you. You should contact the facility to ask about setting up a phone account for your loved one.

   Similarly, call the facility for information on how to send your loved one money if you want them to have funds to purchase basic necessities or food.

4 *Report Any Raids*

   Write down details about what happened as soon as possible.

   Find the reporting non-profit in your state. In North Carolina, call La Migra at 336-543-0353.

5 *Gather Immigration and Criminal Documents, If Any*

   Collect any prior immigration application filed and receipt notice.

   Collect police reports, probable cause affidavits, charging documents, and sentencing documents.

6 *Locate Immigration Court Hearing Information*

   Using the A#, you can find their next immigration court hearing here: acis.eoir.justice.gov/en/

   You can also call 1-800-898-7180.

Finding an Attorney or Representative

Immigration law is complicated. Check with your state bar association and the list of currently disciplined immigration practitioners to make sure the representative is in good standing. See links to the following directories in the endnotes of this book:

In North Carolina
justia.com/lawyers/immigration-law/north-carolina

Nationally
justice.gov/eoir/list-of-currently-disciplined-practitioners

SOURCE: National Immigrant Justice Center

City / County / State Government

On Tuesday, January 27, 2026, Washington State Governor Bob Ferguson and Attorney General Nick Brown denounced ICE activities in Minnesota and presented a proactive plan for Washington State to deal with the ICE incursion. (Office of the Governor of Washington)

On October 6, 2025, Chicago mayor Brandon Johnson signed an "Anti-ICE Zone" Executive Order which created clear mechanisms to prohibit federal immigration agents from using any City-owned property in their ongoing operations in Chicago. The order expanded upon Mayor Johnson's Protecting Chicago initiative, inviting local businesses and community organizations to join the citywide effort to safeguard communities, while advancing measures to rein in the reckless behavior of federal immigration agents. (Office of the Mayor of Chicago)

"We will not tolerate ICE agents violating our residents' constitutional rights nor will we allow the federal government to disregard our local authority. ICE agents are detaining elected officials, tear-gassing protestors, children, and Chicago police officers, and abusing Chicago residents. We will not stand for that in our city," said Mayor Johnson. "With this Executive Order, Chicago stands firm in protecting the Constitutional rights of our residents and immigrant communities and upholding our democracy." (City of Chicago)

Now is the time to approach your local and State governments to demand a plan for a possible ICE incursion. You can do this by calling, writing letters or, more effectively, showing up at City Council and County government meetings to ask what their plan is if ICE paramilitary vehicles roll through the streets.

IN THE STREETS

Right of Assembly

The First Amendment

"Congress shall make no law respecting an establishment of religion, or prohibiting the free exercise thereof; or abridging the freedom of speech, or of the press; or the right of the people peaceably to assemble, and to petition the Government for a redress of grievances."

The right of assembly was first before the Supreme Court in 1876 in *United States v. Cruikshank.* The Court's dicta broadly declared the outlines of the right of assembly:

"The right of the people peaceably to assemble for the purpose of petitioning Congress for a redress of grievances, or for anything else connected with the powers or the duties of the National Government, is an attribute of national citizenship, and, as such, under the protection of, and guaranteed by, the United States. The very idea of a government, republican in form, implies a right on the part of its citizens to meet peaceably for consultation in respect to public affairs and to petition for a redress of grievances. If it had been alleged in these counts that the object of the defendants was to prevent a meeting for such a purpose, the case would have been within the statute, and within the scope of the sovereignty of the United States."

ADAPTED FROM: Constitution Annotated

Your Rights of Assembly

1   You don't need a permit to protest in response to breaking news.

    You don't need a permit to march in the streets or along sidewalks, as long as you're not obstructing traffic or access to buildings.

2   When you are lawfully present in a public space, you have the right to photograph anything in plain view, including federal buildings and federal agents.

3 If you believe your rights have been violated, when you can, write down everything you remember, get contact information for witnesses, and take photographs of any injuries.

4 If you get stopped by police or federal agents, ask if you are free to go. If they say yes, calmly walk away.

5 If you get arrested, you have the right to ask why. Otherwise, say you wish to remain silent and ask for a lawyer immediately. Don't sign, say or agree to anything without a lawyer present.

6 If you get stopped by a member of the military or any law enforcement officer at a protest, you have the right to remain silent or to tell them that you'll only answer questions in the presence of an attorney—no matter your citizenship or immigration status.

SOURCE: ACLU

Participating in a Protest

What to Bring

Water In your own plastic bottle with a squirt top (to drink and to wash off your skin or eyes).

Backpack or drawstring bag Rather than an over-the-shoulder or a cross-body bag—in case you need to run.

Identification And/or emergency contact information (consider writing this on your skin)

Cash For food and transportation or cash bail, in case you are arrested. Check how much bail is in your location.

Inhaler / medication EpiPen, and several days of prescription medication, in case you are arrested.

Medical alert bracelet Or information about any chronic health conditions or allergies.

Change of clothes In case you are exposed to chemical irritants.

SOURCE: Physicians for Human Rights

What to Wear to Protect Against Chemical Agents

If you have underlying conditions or other vulnerabilities to chemical irritants, weigh your risks carefully as you decide if, when, and where to protest. There are other ways you can assist besides attending demonstrations.

Facemask Scarves and bandannas large enough to cover your face from nose to chin can serve as a substitute.

Shatter-resistant eye protection (E.g. shatter resistant sunglasses, swim googles, or a gas mask.)

Clothing Covering all your skin as much as possible.

Shoes Comfortable, closed, protective shoes that you can run in.

Avoid wearing contact lenses Which can trap irritating chemicals, such as tear gas powder, underneath. If you do wear contact lenses, keep a full facial gas mask or googles on at all times.

Avoid wearing makeup Such as eyeliner, for the same reason.

SOURCE: Physicians for Human Rights

How to Get Rid of a Chemical Irritant

Change your clothes as soon as possible. Rinse your body as soon as you can. Take off your clothes and shoes outside your home to avoid bring any powder indoors.

Hang exposed clothes in an open, ventilated area for at least 48 hours before washing them. If you are not able to keep them in an open place, store them in a sealed bag until they are ready to be washed. Do not mix them with uncontaminated garments, as CS powder can be active for as long as 5 days after being released.

Take a cold shower for at least 20 minutes to prevent the chemicals from irritating your skin any further. Do your best not to breathe in any more tear gas during the shower, and keep your eyes closed. Wash your hair especially well.

If you're still having issues 30 minutes or so after getting all the agents off, are having lung or eye issues, or at all concerned about your exposure, seek medical care.

SOURCE: Physicians for Human Rights

Optional Additional Equipment

Bicycle Helmet Protect your Head!

Bandanna One that is wet should filter enough gas to help you escape. (A 2009 Pentagon report mentions that a bandanna soaked in lemon juice could mitigate the effects of tear gas.)

Respirators and Gas Masks Crimethinc has a guide to these.

Sealed Eyewear Check out the guide above.

Your Phone For filming.

Filming ICE

Here are three things to know about filming the police:

› You can take pictures of anything in plain view in a public space including federal buildings, transportation facilities, and the police, as long as you are not interfering with law enforcement.

› Police officers may not confiscate or demand to view your digital photographs or video without a warrant, and they cannot delete your photographs or video under any circumstances.

› The Mobile Justice NC app allows you to record audio and video that is then automatically sent to the ACLU of North Carolina. (ACLU of North Carolina) See if there's an applicable app in your area.

Here is what you should do if you are stopped by police because you were taking photos or video:

› Always remain polite and never physically resist a police officer.

› The right question to ask is, "Am I free to go?" If the officer says no, then you are being detained, something that under the law an officer cannot do without reasonable suspicion that you have or are about to commit a crime, or are in the process of doing so. Until you ask to leave, your being stopped is considered voluntary under the law and is legal.

› If you are detained, politely ask what crime you are suspected of committing, and remind the officer that taking photographs is your right under the First Amendment and does not constitute reasonable suspicion of criminal activity.

SOURCE: ACLU of North Carolina

Tips for Filming ICE

› Using a burner or alternate phone can help protect your privacy and the privacy of those around you.

› Turn off all biometrics (fingerprint and face recognition systems) and revert to a numerical password. See page 30.

› Start recording as soon as possible, even before anything 'happens.' This provides necessary context and background information.

› Hold the phone horizontally. This allows a wider area to be captured.

› Don't stop and start, record continuously. This helps to protect against claims the footage has been manipulated in some way.

› If you can, film a 360 degree pan (full circle). This also makes it harder for people to claim the footage isn't real.

› Focus on the ICE agents themselves, rather than using the camera to record those being detained. You want to protect the detainees as much as possible.

› Stay at a safe distance. Do not interfere with the agents.

› Narrate what appears to be happening as calmly as possible.

› Though it may seem tempting, don't post your video immediately on social media. You may endanger people shown in the video. Many ICE resistance organizations have ways of uploading the footage so that it can be reviewed and decisions can be made when, or if, to make the video public. Find out who they are in your area.

› Stay calm. Remember that your primary concern should be for the safety of the detainees, and your own safety. If it's safer to stop filming, stop filming.

SOURCE: *Wired*

On Your Phone and Computer

› Turn off Face ID or fingerprint ID (biometrics) on your phone, especially when there is a risk that you will interact with law enforcement. Police can use these to get into your phone without a warrant. You can turn these off and revert to a numerical password on most phones in Settings. Refer to endnotes for specific steps.

› Get a VPN. Otherwise, everything you click on can identify your location. *Cybernews* has a list of some.

A VPN (Virtual Private Network) provides online privacy and security. With a VPN you can unblock websites, protect sensitive data, and surf the web with peace of mind.

Some browsers have VPN extensions available or, you can download and sign up for others, such as Signal.

› The US government cannot generally view Signal chats, as they are end-to-end encrypted. This means that the information is encrypted and decrypted in the user's browser, making it technically impossible for the app's administrators to access the contents.

However, the government could view the chats if they were leaked or turned over by someone in the Signal chat. Assume that information in a Signal chat could be available to law enforcement.

› Do not use Google Docs or Gmail. In addition to collecting all your personal information, Google saves your data on its servers and scans it for commercial purposes—and who knows what else. There are open-source, privacy-focused tools like CryptPad, which uses end-to-end encryption.

› Learn which apps can identify your location: limit or turn off those sharing permissions. *The Zebra* has a starter list.

› Limit your interactions with people who say, "I don't take precautions, I'm already on a list, I don't have anything on my phone" and the like. They truly may not care for themselves, but they are putting others at risk.

› Use a vetting process for strategy chats to ensure that somebody trustworthy can vouch for everyone who participates.

SOURCE: *Crimethinc*

Minneapolis Tactics

The citizens of Minneapolis, Minnesota, have deployed and perfected a number of tactics to identify, hinder, and protect their neighbors from ICE and CBP. Many of these tactics have been adopted and adapted from ICE Watch Trainings held across the country. If you can, find an ICE watch training in your area and attend. You will be given valuable tools in the fight against ICE, and you will become part of a community with the same concerns.

Resistance to ICE and CBP rests in the local community, whether it's a few neighbors standing on a street corner to alert their immigrant neighbors to danger, or organized actions which bring tens of thousands of people to the streets.

Make no mistake, though non-violent by nature, this work can be dangerous, as the deaths of Alex Pretti and Renee Nicole Good reveal. In addition, rubber bullets have been fired into the faces and bodies of protestors. Flash-bang grenades and tear gas have been tossed into cars. Protestors have been beaten.

You must choose the level of vulnerability you are comfortable with. Not everyone can be everywhere. You are not obligated to do everything.

Setting Up Rapid Response Networks

Rapid Response networks are groups of community members who mobilize for immediate actions. These networks may monitor local ICE offices, and detention and processing centers. Other rapid response teams can appear in the neighborhoods and locations where ICE has been deployed. A good system includes strong communication networks **between** as well as **within** neighborhoods and towns.

Their goal is often three-fold:

› Provide an early warning system about surges and convoys to others in the local rapid response networks.

> To gather data with a special focus on the license plate database (as ICE officers usually use unmarked cars).

> To ensure ICE knows they are being watched, even on their own turf.

Rapid response team members have followed ICE vehicles from their hotels, offices, and staging centers, reporting their probable destinations to other teams.

Rapid response teams use Signal, a free end-to-end encrypted phone and text app. This protects the privacy of those on either end of the call or text.

The city is divided into neighborhood-based zones and team members may be in cars or on foot.

In addition, protests have included:

> Noise protest outside the hotels where ICE officers are staying

> Refusal of service and use of restrooms (See the For Businesses section of this book)

> Blockades of ICE Headquarters and offices

> Non-violent protests

> Constant filming

LRADs (Long Range Acoustic Devices)

At the time of this writing, it appears Minnesota State Troopers have deployed Long Range Acoustic Devices to assert control over protestors in Minneapolis. (*CBS*) LRADs can be used as a sonic weapon and can cause nausea, vomiting, and permanent hearing loss.

LRADs produce high-frequency, highly directional sound to disperse crowds. They can create enough sound pressure to burst eardrums. The longer you are subjected to the sound, the more severe the damage to your hearing may be.

LRADs create a "beam," much like a spotlight, and the best safety measure is to get out of their "beam," as far away and as quickly as possible.

There's not a lot of advice on protecting yourself from LRADs, except to get out of the way. Earplugs, noise cancelling headphones, etc. are ineffectual. (Reddit)

Riot shields, or other objects with sufficient mass (tables, doors, etc) may work but they may also re-direct the sound to those around you who are unprotected. (Tech Ingredients)

AT HOME

Mutual Aid

Mutual aid is an organizational model where people voluntarily share resources in times of crisis. It's a community-based system which utilizes both non-profits and individuals to meet collective needs.

Mutual aid is about direct care driven by people working within their own and neighboring communities. It is fluid (accessing needs and responding to them) and collaborative.

Organizations

Mutual aid may take the form of supporting (by money, material donations, or volunteer work) non-profit agencies in your area. For those affected by the fear of ICE raids or detention, or those who are reeling from the detention of family member, non-profits agencies could provide:

› Food and medications
› Rent assistance
› Legal assistance

Explore the non-profit agencies in your area, the kind of work they do, and how you might contribute.

Individual

Mutual aid is also neighbors helping neighbors. In Minneapolis, neighbors organized to buy groceries, pick up medications, and supply other necessities to their neighbors, delivering them to their doorstep, as well as rallying if ICE appeared.

Mutual aid is also non-material support: checking in on folks, dropping by for a visit, listening. Americans under threat from ICE can feel isolated and alone.

NOTE: Your neighbors will be naturally suspicious if you've never spoken to them before and suddenly appear at their door, offering to help. Get to know them now.

Boycotts

Boycotts have sometimes proven to be an effective way of forcing corporations to pay the price for colluding with ICE.

You can refuse to patronize corporations through a boycott. You can also write to corporate executives explaining the reason for your boycott.

You can join a protest at a local store or corporate office.

Here is an ongoing list of corporations known to collude with, or support, ICE: wiki.icelist.is

The full list is too long to print here, but includes major corporations, such as Amazon, AT&T, Google, Comcast, Dell, Eastern Airlines, FedEx, Hilton, Home Depot, IBM, Marriott, Microsoft, Pandora, Ring, Spotify, Target, UPS, and many others.

Refusal to Pay Taxes as a Conscientious Objector

One form of resistance being discussed anew is refusing to pay your taxes, or a portion of your taxes, as a Conscientious Objector.

During World War II, 43,000 American men refused to serve in the US Armed Forces. They were mostly from the traditional "Peace" churches. Some served in non-combat roles, some in Civil Service, and some were imprisoned.

However, there is no existing alternative to non-payment of taxes and both the Internal Revenue Service and the courts have repeatedly judged it illegal, subject to fines or imprisonment.

In July of 2021, Rep. James McGovern (D-MA) introduced the Religious Freedom Peace Tax Fund, (HR 4529 of the 117th Congress) which would assure the conscientiously opposed that their taxes would be used for non-military purposes only. The bill has yet to be passed.

SOURCE: National War Tax Resistance
Coordinating Committee and Congress.gov

On the Internet

› Share only posts with documenting links.

› Avoid online discussions or arguments with people you don't know who show up on your feeds.

› Don't join online groups unless you've thoroughly researched them. Be equally suspicious of GoFundMes or other sites purporting to collect money.

› Share only reputable news sources. Be aware legacy media may not be a reputable source.

› Explore US news reported from other countries. Among print publishers that also publish online, *The Guardian* and *Al Jazeera* are well respected.

Travel

At the border, you will likely deal with CBP agents, but you may also encounter Homeland Security Investigations (HSI) agents.

In general, officers may stop people at the border to determine if they are admissible to the US. They may search belongings for contraband, whether they are considered suspicious or not.

Recently, US officials have searched phones and laptops. This is currently a legally contested search. (Again, before you travel, turn off all biometrics on your phone and laptop (see page 30.) ICE and CBP can gain access using your face or thumbprint.

Officers may not, legally, select people for personal search based on your religion, race, national origin, gender ethnicity, or political beliefs. It's not legal, but we know it is happening.

Border officers may ask about your immigration status. If you are a US citizen, you need only answer questions about your identity and citizenship. If you are a non-citizen visa holder, or visitor, you could be denied entry if you refuse to answer questions.

Legally, officers may not ask you about your religious beliefs and political opinions, but these questions have been reported during the second Trump administration.

If you are a US citizen, you do not have to answer these questions, and you cannot legally be denied entry to the US based on that refusal.

If you are a non-citizen visa holder or visitor, you may refuse to answer questions, but it may delay your entry or lead to a possible denial of entry.

Border officers have sometimes asked people to unlock their phones or provide passwords for their laptop.

If you are a US citizen, you cannot be denied entry for refusing to supply passwords or unlock your phone. Refusal, however, could lead to delay, further questioning, or seizure of your device.

If you are a non-citizen or visitor, you may be denied entry for refusal to unlock your phone or supply passwords.

SOURCE: ACLU Pennsylvania and ACLU.org

AS A BUSINESS

Plan for ICE Encounters at Your Business

› Take a Fourth Amendment Workplace Training. SiembraNC offers virtual classes.

› Create plans for what to do and how to respond. A plan would include whether or how to hold agents in the public part of the business (reception area, showroom, serving area), how to let others know ICE has arrived, how to ask for a warrant and what you need to see on the warrant.

› Train your staff not to talk to ICE agents; staff in businesses are not required to answer questions. Make sure someone offsite has a copy of your response plan.

› Practice your plan, just like a fire drill.

› Memorize the name and phone number for immigration lawyers and advocates, and your Congressional Representative and Senators.

› Print out Know Your Rights materials for your employees.

› Always carry valid identification.

› Clearly mark private areas, like back rooms, break rooms, storerooms, offices, and kitchens. Place clear 'Employees Only" or "Private" signs on doors to those spaces and keep them closed, and locked (if possible).

If ICE Enters Your Business

› Remain calm and help your employees to remain calm. Do not run. (This could give ICE reason to detain you.).

› You and your employees have the right to remain silent and refuse to sign documents or answer questions.

› You and your employees do not have to voluntarily reveal anyone's immigration status or show identification.

› You may ask to see a search warrant. ICE can enter public areas of your business, but they generally must have a valid judicial search warrant to enter private areas of your business.

› If they present a warrant, read it. It must be signed by a judge, name your specific business, and specify the area to be searched.

› A deportation warrant is different from a search warrant and does not allow ICE agents to make you take them to employees or enter private areas without permission.

› You can refuse entry into private areas without a search warrant.

› ICE may try to lure you and your employees out of private areas. Unless being detained, ICE cannot make anyone move or stay.

› If ICE agents enter private areas without a search warrant, you may ask for their names and badge numbers and write them down.

Other Business Spaces

As long as it is private property, you can refuse the use of it to ICE agents. This could include parking lots, warehouses, open fields, etc.

Refusing Service to ICE

Many businesses in Minneapolis have refused service to ICE agents. These services have included food, gas, and restroom facilities.

It is legal to refuse services to people who are not a protected class. A protected class includes those covered under religious, racial, or sexual orientation groups.

For instance, a restaurant may refuse to serve alcohol to someone they deem already intoxicated, but cannot refuse service to someone wearing a hijab because they are wearing a hijab.

As an individual employee, you have a right to refuse someone service, but your employer has the right to fire you if they disagree. Ask what the company policy is on refusal.

ICE is not a protected class, but legal opinions vary on whether it is legal to refuse service. As of January 2026, we can find no instance of a business owner arrested for refusing service to ICE. Make your own decision.

SOURCE: Congressional Committee on Small Business

General Strike

During a general strike, non-essential workers refuse to work for the length of the strike, and participating businesses refuse to open. Customers refuse to buy. General strikes have often been effective in other countries.

Most strikes in the US are protected, thus employees are legally allowed to strike. Protected strikes are strikes called to protest:

› Unfair labor practices
› Economic strikes, including disputes over wages or benefits
› Recognition strikes, intended to force employers to recognize unions
› Jurisdictional strikes, which cover union members rights to certain job assignments

SOURCE: H. Sanford Rudnick & Associates

A general strike, involving employees not part of a union or seeking union representation, would usually be considered a "wildcat" or unprotected strike. Participating in an unprotected strike could result in termination or disciplinary action.

As an employer, consider what your policy will be if a general strike is called in your city, state, or nationwide.

As an employee, remember that you could be fired for participating in a general strike. (Nothing prevents you from suddenly feeling sick on the day of the general strike, however.)

IN THE MILITARY / LAW ENFORCEMENT

Illegal Orders

The Uniform Code of Military Justice states that all members have the right, and in some cases the duty, to refuse illegal orders. A member's oath is to the Constitution (which incorporates international treaties ratified by the U.S. on human rights and the law of war), not to the Commander-in-Chief or any other individual in the chain of command.

None of the scenarios below would necessarily involve illegal orders, but these are all actions that the current Commander-In-Chief has discussed publicly as possibilities, which might involve the U.S. military, and that might lead to illegal orders.

It's unclear whether any of these things will happen, but you may want to think about what you would do if you were given orders to take part in any of these military actions or to take specific actions once deployed, since it may not be the deployment itself that's illegal.

In the United States

› Use of military forces to carry out deportations, removals, or detention of immigrants. (Removals to countries where those removed are likely to be tortured could violate the Convention Against Torture, to which the U.S. is a party.)

› Use of military forces against civilian protesters. (The Posse Comitatus Act prohibits the use of federal troops for domestic law enforcement, with certain exceptions, primarily in the event of an insurrection. Thus, one has an arguable duty to refuse to obey an order to assist law enforcement personnel unless there is an "insurrection.")

Outside the United States

› U.S. attacks on vessels in international or foreign waters.

› U.S. attacks on surviving crew or passengers of vessels sunk at sea.

› U.S. invasion of, or attack on, Venezuelan territory, vessels, or nationals.

- › U.S. attack, invasion, or attempt to seize control of the Panama Canal by force.
- › U.S. "preemptive" use of military force against China, Iran, or other countries.
- › U.S. attempt to annex Greenland or to attack or invade Canada.
- › U.S. use of nuclear weapons against China or another country.
- › Torture or mistreatment of civilians, prisoners of war, or other detainees. International law prohibits the use of military force except in retaliation for a military strike or in the face of an imminent military strike. The International Court of Justice has also held that the use of nuclear weapons is a violation of international law, although that ruling is not necessarily binding on US courts. Other treaties govern torture, treatment of detainees, stopping and boarding of vessels in international waters, etc.

The only way to find out if an order is legal or illegal is to obey, or refuse to obey, and see what is decided after by a military court, a civilian court reviewing a military decision, or a war crimes or human rights tribunal.

Disobeying an order could lead to arrest, reassignment, or dishonorable discharge. Some discretion in response rests with your commanding officer. You can read about the ethics of military disobedience at thestrategybridge.org.

If you think an order, or a possible order, might be illegal, know that you are not alone. Other members of the military are also considering these issues. Find organizations that support those who refuse illegal orders at whistlebloweraid.org. Be prepared and plan ahead. Talk with a civilian lawyer. Explore how to report illegal orders at girightshotline.org.

If you obey an illegal order, you could be court-martialed for war crimes or charged with violations of the law.

SOURCE: National Lawyers Guild Military Law Task Force

US GOVERNMENT SIMPLE SABOTAGE FIELD MANUAL

About the Manual

The Simple Sabotage Field Manual was published in January 1944 by the U.S. Office of Strategic Services (OSS) as a guide to aid citizens in combatting fascist forces in other countries. After the Second World War, the OSS was decomissioned and its programs were administered under other government agencies; upon its establishment in 1947, the Central Intelligence Agency assumed many of the functions of the OSS. The following short history is taken directly from the CIA website:

> The rascally spies of OSS knew a thing or two about mischief making, especially when it came to undermining America's enemies in World War II. One of their more imaginative ideas was to train everyday citizens in the art of simple sabotage.
>
> Thus, the "Simple Sabotage Field Manual" was born.
>
> This previously classified booklet describes ways to train normal people to be purposely annoying telephone operators, dysfunctional train conductors, befuddling middle managers, blundering factory workers, unruly movie theater patrons, and so on.
>
> In other words, teaching people to do their jobs badly.
>
> OSS Director William "Wild Bill" Donovan had select parts of the manual declassified and disseminated to citizens of enemy states through pamphlets, targeted radio broadcasts, and in person. (*CIA.gov*)

The introduction to the manual states:

> This Simple Sabotage Field Manual—Strategic Services (Provisional)—is published for the information and guidance of all concerned and will be used as the basic doctrine for Strategic Services training for this subject.

The contents of this Manual should be carefully controlled and should not be allowed to come into unauthorized hands.

The instructions may be placed in separate pamphlets or leaflets according to categories of operations but should be distributed with care and not broadly. They should be used as a basis of radio broadcasts only for local and special cases and as directed by the theater commander.

The manual continues, in its first chapter:

Sabotage varies from highly technical *coup de main* acts that require detailed planning and the use of specially-trained operatives, to innumerable simple acts which the ordinary individual citizen-saboteur can perform. This paper is primarily concerned with the latter type. **Simple sabotage does not require specially prepared tools or equipment; it is executed by an ordinary citizen who may or may not act individually and without the necessity for active connection with an organized group; and it is carried out in such a way as to involve a minimum danger of injury, detection, and reprisal.** [Emphasis added.]

Where destruction is involved, the weapons of the citizen-saboteur are salt, nails, candles, pebbles, thread, or any other materials he might normally be expected to possess as a householder or as a worker in his particular occupation. His arsenal is the kitchen shelf, the trash pile, his own usual kit of tools and supplies. The targets of his sabotage are usually objects to which he has normal and inconspicuous access in everyday life.

A second type of simple sabotage requires no destructive tools whatsoever and produces physical damage, if any, by highly indirect means. It is based on universal opportunities to make faulty decisions, to adopt a noncooperative attitude, and to induce others to follow suit. Making a faulty decision may be simply a matter of placing tools in one spot instead of another. A non-cooperative attitude may involve nothing more than creating an unpleasant situation among one's fellow workers, engaging in bickerings, or displaying surliness and stupidity.

This type of activity, sometimes referred to as the "human element," is frequently responsible for accidents, delays, and general obstruction even under normal conditions. The potential saboteur should discover what types of faulty decisions and the operations are *normally* found in this kind of work and should then devise his sabotage so as to enlarge that "margin for error."

Selections from the Simple Sabotage Manual

The following selection from the *Simple Sabotage Manual* describes non-violent ways to impede an invading force. Not all resistance is overt. Not all resistance is immediately obvious.

Transportation

1. Change sign posts at intersections and forks; the enemy will go the wrong way and it may be miles before he discovers his mistakes. In areas where traffic is composed primarily of enemy autos, trucks, and motor convoys of various kinds remove danger signals from curves and intersections.
2. When the enemy asks for directions, give him wrong information. Especially when enemy convoys are in the neighborhood, truck drivers can spread rumors and give false information about bridges being out, ferries closed, and detours lying ahead.
3. If you can start damage to a heavily traveled road, passing traffic and the elements will do the rest. Construction gangs can see that too much sand or water is put in concrete or that the road foundation has soft spots. Anyone can scoop ruts in asphalt and macadam roads which turn soft in hot weather; passing trucks will accentuate the ruts to a point where substantial repair will be needed. Dirt roads also can be scooped out. If you are a road laborer, it will be only a few minutes work to divert a small stream from a sluice so that it runs over and eats away the road.
4. Distribute broken glass, nails, and sharp rocks on roads to puncture tires.

ICE and CBP agents will be using apps on their phone to navigate, but they could stop you to ask for directions or other mundane questions. You could choose not to answer at all, or you could give them bad information which might delay them.

Sabotaging roads or vehicles is obviously illegal, so weigh the risks before you attempt that type of action.

*

Feigned incompetence, confusion, or lack of talent cannot be underestimated in a movement of resistance.

If you work for an organization that interfaces or collaborates with ICE, you can resist by following some of the guidelines below, excerpted from the *Simple Sabotage Manual.*

General Interference with Organizations and Production: In Organizations and At Conferences

1 Insist on doing everything through "channels." Never permit short-cuts to be taken in order to expedite decisions.
2 Make "speeches." Talk as frequently as possible and at great length. Illustrate your "points" by long anecdotes and accounts of personal experiences. Never hesitate to make a few appropriate "patriotic" comments.
3 When possible, refer all matters to committees, for "further study and consideration." Attempt to make the committees as large as possible—never less than five.
4 Bring up irrelevant issues as frequently as possible.
5 Haggle over precise wordings of communications, minutes, resolutions.
6 Refer back to matters decided upon at the last meeting and attempt to re-open the question of the advisability of that decision.
7 Advocate "caution." Be "reasonable" and urge your fellow-conferees to be "reasonable" and avoid haste which might result in embarrassments or difficulties later on.
8 Be worried about the propriety of any decision—raise the question of whether such action as is contemplated lies within the jurisdiction of the group or whether it might conflict with the policy of some higher echelon.

*General Interference with Organizations
and Production: For Employees*

1 *Work slowly.* Think out ways to increase the number
   of movements necessary on your job: use a light
   hammer instead of a heavy one, try to make a small
   wrench do when a big one is necessary, use little
   force where considerable force is needed, and so on.

2 Contrive as many interruptions to your work as you
   can: when changing the material on which you are
   working, as you would on a lathe or punch, take need-
   less time to do it. If you are cutting, shaping or doing
   other measured work, measure dimensions twice as
   often as you need to. When you go to the lavatory,
   spend a longer time there than is necessary. Forget
   tools so that you will have to go back after them.

3 Even if you understand the language, pretend not
   to understand instructions in a foreign tongue.

4 Pretend that instructions are hard to understand,
   and ask to have them repeated more than once.
   Or pretend that you are particularly anxious to
   do your work, and pester the foreman with un-
   necessary questions.

5 Do your work poorly and blame it on bad tools, ma-
   chinery, or equipment. Complain that these things
   are preventing you from doing your job right.

6 Never pass on your skill and experience to a new
   or less skillful worker.

7 Snarl up administration in every possible way. Fill out
   forms illegibly so that they will have to be done over;
   make mistakes or omit requested information in forms.

8 If possible, join or help organize a group for presenting
   employee problems to the management. See that the
   procedures adopted are as inconvenient as possible
   for the management, involving the presence of a large
   number of employees at each presentation, entailing

more than one meeting for each grievance, bringing up problems which are largely imaginary, and so on.

In our context: you might work for a hotel which houses ICE agents and you may feel, for whatever reason, that you could not refuse to serve them. However, you could:

› *Work slowly.* Take as long as possible to complete any task.
› *Make mistakes.* Confuse the reservations, mix up the key cards, get their room service orders wrong.
› *Give them bad or confusing information.* If they ask about the closest restaurant or gas station, send them in the other direction.

General Devices for Lowering
Morale and Creating Confusion

1 Give lengthy and incomprehensible explanations when questioned.
2 Report imaginary spies or danger to the Gestapo or police.
3 Act stupid.
4 Be as irritable and quarrelsome as possible without getting yourself into trouble.
5 Misunderstand all sorts of regulations concerning such matters as rationing, transportation, traffic regulations.
6 Complain against ersatz materials.
7 In public treat axis nationals or quislings coldly.
8 Stop all conversation when axis nationals or quislings enter a cafe.
9 Cry and sob hysterically at every occasion, especially when confronted by government clerks.
10 Boycott all movies, entertainments, concerts, newspapers which are in any way connected with the quisling authorities.

The value in acting stupid cannot be underestimated.

ENDNOTES

Online documents of the US Government have been notoriously unstable during the Trump Administration. Pages, data, and websites have disappeared without warning. Every effort has been made to reference reputable sites in the compilation of this book, but some government sites or pages could vanish. The Internet Archive or The Wayback Machine could be the best tool for recovery.

2   USA Facts. "What is ICE and what does it do?" usafacts.org/articles/what-is-ice-and-what-does-it-do

2   *The Seattle Times.* "ICE and Border Patrol: What is the difference?" www.seattletimes.com/seattle-news/ice-and-border-patrol-what-is-the-difference/

3   Office of Homeland Security Statistics. "Table 39. Aliens Removed or Returned: Fiscal Years 1892 to 2019." ohss.dhs.gov/topics/immigration/yearbook/2019/table39

4   Migration Policy Institute. "Trump's First Year on Immigration Policy: Rhetoric vs. Reality." migrationpolicy.org/research/trump-first-year-immigration-policy-rhetoric-vs-reality

4   Migration Policy Institute. "Comparing the Biden and Trump Deportation Records." migrationpolicy.org/article/biden-deportation-record

5   *Politico.* "We watched 20 Trump rallies. His racist, anti-immigrant messaging is getting darker." politico.com/news/2024/10/12/trump-racist-rhetoric-immigrants-00183537

5   *Reuters.* "Trump set to expand immigration crackdown in 2026 despite brewing backlash." reuters.com/world/us/trump-set-expand-immigration-crackdown-2026-despite-brewing-backlash-2025-12-21/

6 *NPR.* "How Trump's tax cut and policy bill aims to 'supercharge' immigration enforcement." npr.org/2025/07/03/g-s1-75609/big-beautiful-bill-ice-funding-immigration

6 *NPR.* "How ICE grew to be the highest-funded U.S. law enforcement agency." npr.org/2026/01/21/nx-s1-5674887/ice-budget-funding-congress-trump

6 USAJOBS. "Deportation Officer." ice.usajobs.gov/job/853993800

6 U.S. Immigration and Customs Enforcement. "ICE announces most successful federal law enforcement agency recruitment campaign in American history." ice.gov/news/releases/ice-announces-most-successful-federal-law-enforcement-agency-recruitment-campaign

6 CBC. "ICE nodding to far-right extremists in recruitment posts, experts say." cbc.ca/news/ice-recruiting-9.7058294

6 *The Nation.* "Whom Is ICE Actually Recruiting?" thenation.com/article/society/ice-recruitment-white-supremacists/

7 *Slate.* "You've Heard About Who ICE Is Recruiting. The Truth Is Far Worse. I'm the Proof." slate.com/news-and-politics/2026/01/ice-recruitment-minneapolis-shooting.html

7 *The Oregonian.* "A former Portland journalist says she was hired by ICE after 6-minute interview." oregonlive.com/news/2026/01/a-former-portland-journalist-says-she-was-hired-by-ice-after-6-minute-interview.html

7 Poynter Institute. "How a 47-day ICE training claim spread—and what the record actually shows." poynter.org/fact-checking/2026/ice-47-days-training-reduced-trump/

7 *Al-Jazeera.* "What ICE agents are taught: How to use 'deadly force', evade lawsuits." aljazeera.com/features/2026/1/23/are-ice-agents-trained-to-shoot-and-evade-lawsuits

7 *Axios.* "New data: ICE arrests surge as agency chases Trump quota." axios.com/2025/12/04/trump-ice-immigration-arrests-deportations

8 ACLU. "Fight for Immigrants' Rights." aclu.org/news/immigrants-rights/inside-an-ice-detention-center-detained-people-describe-severe-medical-neglect-harrowing-conditions

8   Amnesty International. "USA: New Findings Reveal Human Rights Violations." amnesty.org/en/latest/news/2025/12/estados-unidos-nuevas-investigaciones-revelan-violaciones-de-derechos-humanos-en-los-centros-de-detencion-de-alligator-alcatraz-y-krome-en-florida/

8   Physicians for Human Rights. "'Endless Nightmare': Torture and Inhuman Treatment in Solitary Confinement." phr.org/our-work/resources/endless-nightmare-solitary-confinement-in-us-immigration-detention/

8   *Reuters.* "Four died in ICE custody this week as 2025 deaths reach 20-year high." reuters.com/world/us/four-died-ice-custody-this-week-2025-deaths-reach-20-year-high-2025-12-19/

8   ABC News. "Trump wants to send US citizens to foreign prisons. Legal experts say he can't." congress.gov/119/meeting/house/118339/documents/HHRG-119-GO00-20250605-SD007.pdf

8   Human Rights Watch. "Declaration on prison conditions in El Salvador." hrw.org/news/2025/03/20/human-rights-watch-declaration-prison-conditions-el-salvador-jgg-v-trump-case

9   Cornell Law School. "Due process." law.cornell.edu/wex/due_process

9   *NPR.* "Trump wants to bypass immigration courts. Experts warn it's a 'slippery slope.'" npr.org/2025/04/29/g-s1-63187/trump-courts-immigration-judges-due-process

9   *Reason Magazine.* "Judge Says ICE Violated Court Orders in 74 Cases." reason.com/2026/01/30/judge-says-ice-violated-court-orders-in-74-cases-see-them-all-here/

10 *CNN.* "New ICE policy allows officers to enter homes without a judge's warrant." cnn.com/2026/01/22/politics/ice-memo-warrantless-entry-what-we-know

10 *Axios.* "Judge orders ICE to release 300+ detained immigrants." axios.com/local/chicago/2025/11/12/ice-release-300-detained-immigrants

10 *Axios.* "New data: ICE arrests surge as agency chases Trump quota." axios.com/2025/12/04/trump-ice-immigration-arrests-deportations

11 The Marshall Project. "ICE Threw Thousands of Kids in Detention." themarshallproject.org/2025/12/17/children-immigration-detention-dilley-ice

11 *The Guardian.* "2025 was ICE's deadliest year in two decades." theguardian.com/us-news/ng-interactive/2026/jan/04/ice-2025-deaths-timeline

11 *Al-Jazeera.* "US witnessed many ICE-related deaths in 2026." aljazeera.com/news/2026/1/27/us-witnessed-many-ice-related-deaths-in-2026-here-are-their-stories

13 X.com. "DHS law enforcement has made OVER 900 ARRESTS." x.com/DHSgov/status/1973796727615598738

13 *ProPublica.* "'I Lost Everything.'" propublica.org/article/chicago-venezuela-immigration-ice-fbi-raids-no-criminal-charges

13 Facebook.com. "Masked up, mission ready." facebook.com/reel/3186222231556535

13 *The Assembly.* "Greg Bovino's Last Stand." theassemblync.com/news/politics/greg-bovino-border-patrol-immigration

14 *The Guardian.* "ICE detains five-year-old Minnesota boy arriving home, say school officials." theguardian.com/us-news/2026/jan/21/ice-arrests-five-year-old-boy-minnesota

17 SiembraNC. siembranc.org/

18 Crimethinc. "When the Feds Come to Your City." crimethinc.com/2025/12/03/when-the-feds-come-to-your-city-standing-up-to-ice-a-guide-from-chicago-organizers

19 4th Amendment Workplaces. 4thworkplace.org.

21 National Immigrant Justice Center. "What to Do if You or a Loved One is Detained." immigrantjustice.org/for-immigrants/know-your-rights/what-do-if-you-or-loved-one-detained

22 Office of the Governor of Washington. "Gov. Ferguson, AG Brown denounce unconstitutional actions." governor.wa.gov/news/2026/governor-ferguson-attorney-general-brown-denounce-unconstitutional-actions-out-control-ice-agents

22 Office of the Mayor of Chicago. "Mayor Johnson Signs 'ICE Free Zone" Executive Order." chicago.gov/city/en/depts/

mayor/press_room/press_releases/2025/october/city-property-executive-order.html

22 City of Chicago. "Executive Order No. 2025–8." chicity-clerk.s3.us-west-2.amazonaws.com/s3fs-public-1/reports/EXECUTIVE%20ORDER%202025-8.pdf

24 Constitution Annotated. "Doctrine on Freedoms of Assembly and Petition." constitution.congress.gov/browse/essay/amdt1-10-2/ALDE_00000223/

25 ACLU. "Protesters' Rights." aclu.org/know-your-rights/protesters-rights

26 Physicians for Human Rights. "Preparing for, Protecting Against, and Treating Tear Gas." phr.org/our-work/resources/preparing-for-protecting-against-and-treating-tear-gas-and-other-chemical-irritant-exposure-a-protesters-guide/

27 Ibid.

27 Ibid.

27 Crimethinc. "A Demonstrator's Guide to Gas Masks and Goggles." crimethinc.com/2020/09/02/a-demonstrators-guide-to-gas-masks-and-goggles-everything-you-need-to-know-to-protect-your-eyes-and-lungs-from-gas-and-projectiles

28 ACLU of NC. "Federal Agents in North Carolina." acluofnorthcarolina.org/news/you-have-right-film-police/

29 *Wired.* "How to Film ICE." wired.com/story/how-to-film-ice

30 Android Central. "How to disable biometrics on your Android phone from the lock screen." androidcentral.com/apps-software/how-to-disable-biometrics-on-your-android-phone-from-the-lock-screen

30 IPhone User Guide. "Change Face ID and attention settings on iPhone." support.apple.com/guide/iphone/change-face-id-and-attention-settings-iph646624222/ios

30 Cybernews. "Best VPNs for the USA." us.cybernews.com/lp/best-vpn-us/

30 The Zebra. "What map apps track (and how to get them to stop)." thezebra.com/resources/driving/what-map-apps-track/

31 Crimethinc. "When the Feds Come to Your City." crimethinc.com/2025/12/03/when-the-feds-come-to-your-city-standing-up-to-ice-a-guide-from-chicago-organizers

34 *CBS.* "Minnesota State Patrol uses long range acoustic device." cbsnews.com/minnesota/news/minnesota-state-patrol-long-range-acoustic-device/

35 Reddit. "How to Protect Yourself from Long Range Acoustic Devices (LRAD)." reddit.com/r/videos/comments/1q0g-f9m/how_to_protect_yourself_from_long_range_acoustic/

35 Tech Ingredients. "Defeating LRAD." youtube.com/watch?v=CXKTBQBugIA

37 National War Tax Resistance Coordinating Committee. "Tax Refusal as Conscientious Objection to War." nwtrcc.org/war-tax-resistance-resources/readings/tax-refusal-as-conscientious-objection-to-war/

37 Congress. "H.R. 4529. Religious Freedom Peace Tax Fund Act." congress.gov/bill/117th-congress/house-bill/4529/text

40 ACLU Pennsylvania. "Know Your Rights While Traveling." aclupa.org/know-your-rights/know-your-rights-while-traveling

40 ACLU. "Fight for the Right to Privacy." aclu.org/news/privacy-technology/can-border-agents-search-your-electronic

44 Congressional Committee on Small Business. "Know Your Rights as a Small Business." https://mcgarvey.house.gov/imo/media/doc/SB%20KYR%20ENG.pdf

45 H. Sanford Rudnick & Associates. "Four Types of Strikes Are Protected Under the NLRB Act." theunionexpert.com/four-types-of-strikes-are-protected-under-the-nlrb-act

49 National Lawyers Guild Military Law Task Force. "FAQ on Refusing Illegal Orders." nlgmltf.org/military-law/2025/faq-on-refusing-illegal-orders/

52 CIA. "The Art of Simple Sabotage." cia.gov/stories/story/the-art-of-simple-sabotage/

52 CIA. "Simple Sabotage Field Manual." cia.gov/static/5c875f3ec660e092cf893f60b4a288df/SimpleSabotage.pdf

FURTHER READING

A short list of recommended reading includes:

Nineteen Eighty-Four. George Orwell (1949)

The Origins of Totalitarianism. Hannah Arendt (1951)

The Devil's Highway. Luis Alberto Urrea (2004)

Democracy in Chains: The Deep History of the Radical Right's Stealth Plan for America. Nancy MacLean (2017)

Fascism Today: What It Is and How to End It. Shane Burley (2017)

On Tyranny: Twenty Lessons from the Twentieth Century. Timothy Snyder (2017)

Dear America: Notes of an Undocumented Citizen. Jose Antonio Vargas (2018)

Democracy May Not Exist, but We'll Miss It When It's Gone. Astra Taylor (2019)

Democracy in One Book or Less: How It Works, Why It Doesn't, and Why Fixing It Is Easier Than You Think. David Litt (2020)

Evil Geniuses: The Unmaking of America; A Recent History. Kurt Andersen (2020)

Long Time Coming: Reckoning with Race in America. Michael Eric Dyson (2020)

Mutual Aid: Building Solidarity During This Crisis (and the Next). Dean Spade (2020)

Stakes is High: Life after the American Dream. Mychal Denzel Smith (2020)

The Undocumented Americans. Kara Cornejo Villavicencio (2020)

Why Didn't We Riot? A Black Man in Trumpland. Issac J. Bailey (2020)

Wilmington's Lie: The Murderous Coup of 1898 and the Rise of White Supremacy. David Zucchino (2020)

The Third Reconstruction: How a Moral Movement Is Overcoming the Politics of Division and Fear. William J. Barber II and Jonathan Wilson Hartgrove (2022)

Solidarity: The Past, Present, and Future of a World-Changing Idea. Leah Hunt-Hendrix and Astra Taylor (2023)

Everyone Who is Gone is Here. Jonathan Blitzer (2024)

Copaganda: How Police and the Media Manipulate Our News. Alec Karakatsanis (2025)

The Cost of Being Undocumented: One Woman's Reckoning with America's Inhumane Math. Alix Dick and Antero Garcia (2025)

Salt in the Snow: A Somali Immigrant Story. Sahra Noor (Publishes June 2026)

www.ingramcontent.com/pod-product-compliance
Lightning Source LLC
Chambersburg PA
CBHW070029030426
42335CB00017B/2354